SINNERS
in the
HANDS
of an
ANGRY GOD

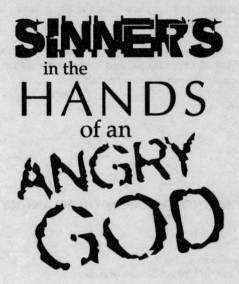

SINNERS
in the
HANDS
of an
ANGRY GOD

JONATHAN EDWARDS

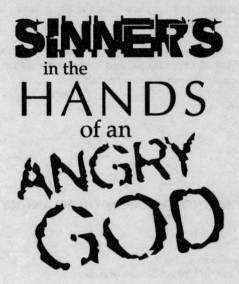 Whitaker House

All Scripture quotations are from the King James Version (KJV) of the Bible.

Editor's note: This book has been edited for the modern reader. Words, expressions, and sentence structure have been updated for clarity and readability.

SINNERS IN THE HANDS OF AN ANGRY GOD

ISBN: 0-88368-415-2
Printed in the United States of America
© 1997 by Whitaker House

Whitaker House
30 Hunt Valley Circle
New Kensington, PA 15068
web site: www.whitakerhouse.com

5 6 7 8 9 10 11 12 13 14 / 10 09 08 07 06 05 04 03 02

Contents

Introduction

Jonathan Edwards was never a man to evade a problem, especially one that concerned the fate of a man's soul. Rather, he was one of the most honest expositors of his time, and to this day he is considered one of the greatest philosophers, if not the greatest, that America has ever produced. His writings and sermons contain some of the most accessible words ever written or spoken on most of the major doctrines of Christianity.

Born in East Windsor, Connecticut, in 1703, Edwards was the only son of the Reverend Timothy Edwards and Esther Stoddard Edwards. He was a dedicated student and scholar from his early youth, well before he entered Yale University at the age of thirteen. Despite his scholarly bent, however, he was also philosophical, and he had an appetite for the divine; his academics never took a higher place than his devotion to God.

In 1729, after earning a Master of Divinity from Yale, Edwards succeeded his grandfather, the famed Solomon Stoddard, as full pastor of the First Church of Northampton, Massachusetts. In the twenty-four years that he lived in Northampton, Edwards was deeply concerned with the nature of true religion. Although only three or four generations had passed since the Puritans had come to the New World, the religious fervor of the church had more or less evaporated. Both thinking and living had fallen to a lower plane. In such an atmosphere, Edwards knew that sinners would never choose to serve and glorify God unless God changed their hearts and planted in them the desire to seek Him.

Therefore, true religion was, and is, a matter of the heart. It is what Dr. Martyn Lloyd-Jones, in his address, "Jonathan Edwards and the Crucial

Importance of Revival," referred to as "a living meeting with God." It is something that must be lived out. Edwards was keenly aware of this, and he set forth to transform his congregation, as well as congregations throughout New England, from "mere believers who understood the logic of Christian doctrine to converted Christians who were genuinely moved by the principles of their belief."[1]

There was one congregation, in Enfield, Connecticut, that was especially unswayed by the message of the Gospel. The people of this district had been more or less unaffected during the Great Awakening of 1734–35 in New England; what is more, they did not seem to mind. Edwards was invited by the pastor at Enfield to bring the work of Christ to this unyielding congregation, and to arouse them through his

---

[1] *The Norton Anthology of American Literature,* shorter edition (New York: W. W. Norton & Co., 1980), 76.

preaching to seek the God that they had been avoiding for so long.

On July 8, 1741, filled, as usual, with a profound sense of the heinousness of sin, Jonathan Edwards preached America's most famous sermon, "Sinners in the Hands of an Angry God," to that congregation at Enfield. His aim was to bring his listeners to at least some realization of the horror of their state: they were objects of God's great displeasure, for they had offended and outraged Him by turning away from His incredible goodness in intervening for their salvation.

"Sinners in the Hands of an Angry God" is saturated with vivid images of the dangers of unforgiven sin and the terrors of being lost. The response of the Enfield church to these images was nothing less than amazing: Edwards was interrupted many times before he finished by people moaning and crying out, "What shall I do to be saved?" The Spirit of God was at work through the life and vitality of Edwards' preaching.

However, shortly after that life-changing day in July, 1741, the sermon underwent heavy criticism, and, to this day, some people still criticize Edwards for simply saying what the Scriptures say. Edwards did say some very alarming things, yet his words were meant only to bring people to understand the truth of their condition. "Sinners in the Hands of an Angry God" was a word of light imparted to darkened souls.

In spite of whatever criticism Edwards' sermon has endured, its light is unobscured after over two hundred and fifty years; the earnestness of his words is not muted at all. Presented here in a format geared especially toward today's reader, "Sinners in the Hands of an Angry God" is as arresting and awakening as it was at Enfield. Edwards' intellect, fired by the Holy Spirit, takes us to the place where man comes face to face with the living God.

True religion is an experience of the heart. To Edwards, the true Christian had not only a knowledge and understanding of the facts of Scripture, but also a renewed sense of divine beauty, holiness, and truth. This is what is needed in the church today: true Christians practicing true religion. A radical change of heart, brought to the people of Enfield by the words of Edwards' sermon, can be brought to fruition even now. May the following words create and elevate within us a desire to practice true Christianity, to the glory of our God.

CHAPTER ONE

The State of Humankind

Their foot shall slide in due time.
    —Deuteronomy 32:35

In this verse, the vengeance of God is threatened on the wicked, unbelieving Israelites, who were God's visible people and who lived under the means of grace,[1] but who, notwithstanding all God's wonderful works toward them, remained "void of counsel," having no understanding in them

---

[1] Means of grace: the Ten Commandments. For Protestants following the Westminster Confession (1646), the "means of grace" consist of the "preaching of the word and the administration of the sacraments of baptism and the Lord's Supper."

(verse 28). Under all the cultivations of heaven, they brought forth bitter and poisonous fruit, as in two verses that precede our text:

> *For their vine is of the vine of Sodom, and of the fields of Gomorrah: their grapes are grapes of gall, their clusters are bitter: their wine is the poison of dragons, and the cruel venom of asps.*
> *(Deuteronomy 32:32–33)*

The Punishment of the Israelites

The phrase I have chosen for my text, "Their foot shall slide in due time," seems to imply the following things. Each of these four implications relates to the punishment and destruction to which these wicked Israelites were exposed.

Prone to Destruction

First of all, the Israelites were always exposed to destruction, just as one who stands or walks in slippery places is always prone to a fall. This is implied in the manner in which their destruction was to come upon them, for it is represented by their foot sliding. The same idea is expressed in Psalm 73:18: "Surely thou didst set them in slippery places: thou castedst them down into destruction."

Exposed to the Unexpected

Second, the phrase implies that they were always exposed to sudden and unexpected destruction. The man who walks in slippery places is at every moment liable to fall. He cannot foresee whether he will stand one moment or fall the next; and when he does fall, he falls at once, without warning. This is also expressed in the seventy-third Psalm:

Surely thou didst set them in slippery places: thou castedst them down into destruction.

> *How are they brought into deso-*
> *lation, as in a moment!*
> *(Psalm 73:18–19)*

Liable because of Themselves

Another thing implied by the text is that they are liable to fall of themselves, without being thrown down by the hand of another. In the same way, one who stands or walks on slippery ground needs nothing but his own weight to throw him down.

At God's Mercy

Fourth, the reason why they have not fallen already and do not fall now, is only that God's appointed time has not yet come. For it is written that, when that due time, or appointed time, comes, "their foot shall slide" (Deuteronomy 32:35).

At that time, they will be left to fall, as they are inclined by their own weight. God will not hold them up in these slippery places any longer, but will let them go. And then, at that very instant, they will fall into destruction, just as he who stands on such slippery, declining ground, on the edge of a pit, cannot stand alone; for when he is let go, he immediately falls and is lost.

The Mere Pleasure of God

From this, observe what our text means: There is nothing that keeps wicked men out of hell, at any one moment, except the mere pleasure of God. By "the mere pleasure of God," I mean His sovereign pleasure, His all-powerful will, restrained by no obligation, hindered by no manner of difficulty; nothing else but God's sovereign will has a hand in the preservation of wicked men. The truth of this observation may become clear through the following considerations.

The Omnipotent God

First, there is no lack of power in God to cast wicked men into hell at any moment. Men's hands cannot be strong when God rises up. The strongest have no power to resist Him, nor can any man escape from His hands. He is not only able to cast wicked men into hell, but He can most easily do it.

Sometimes an earthly ruler finds it very difficult to subdue a rebel who has found means to fortify himself and has made himself strong by having great numbers of followers. However, it is not so with God. There is no fortress that is any defense from the power of God. Though hand join in hand, and vast multitudes of God's enemies combine and associate themselves, they are easily broken into pieces. They are as great heaps of chaff before the whirlwind (see Isaiah 17:13), or large quantities of dry stubble before devouring flames. (See Nahum 1:10.)

We find it easy to tread on and crush a worm that we see crawling on the ground. It is just as easy for us to cut or singe a slender thread by which something hangs. Now, think of how

18

easy it is for God, whenever He pleases, to cast His enemies down to hell. What are we, that we should think we can stand before Him, at whose rebuke the earth trembles, and before whom the rocks are thrown down? (See Nahum 1:4–6.)

The Sword of Justice

The second consideration is that sinners *deserve* to be cast into hell. Divine justice never stands in the way of God using His power at any moment to destroy them; it makes no objection whatsoever. Rather, justice calls aloud for an infinite punishment of their sins. Divine justice says of the tree that brings forth fruit like that of the poisonous grapes of Sodom, "Cut it down; why cumbereth it the ground?" (Luke 13:7). The sword of divine justice is every moment brandished over their heads, and it is nothing but the hand of all-powerful mercy, and God's sovereign will, that holds it back.

A Sentence to Hell

Third, sinners are already under a sentence of condemnation to hell. They not only justly deserve to be cast down to that place, but the sentence of the law of God—that eternal and immutable rule of righteousness that God has fixed between Himself and humankind—has also gone out against them, and stands against them, so that they are already bound over to hell.

Consider what is written in the book of John: "He that believeth not is condemned already" (John 3:18). Every unconverted man properly belongs to hell; that is his place; his nature is from there. "Ye are from beneath," said Christ (John 8:23). And the sinner is bound to that place, for hell is the place assigned to him by justice, by God's Word, and by the sentence of His unchangeable law.

The Objects of God's Wrath

Fourth, let us consider that sinners are the objects of that very same anger and wrath of God that is expressed in the torments of hell. The reason that sinners do not go down to hell, at each moment, is not because God, in whose power they are, is not then very angry with them.

He is angry with many miserable creatures now tormented in hell, all of whom feel and bear the fierceness of His wrath there. Yet, God is much angrier with great numbers of people who are now on earth. In fact, He is angrier with many who are now in the congregations of our churches, many who seem to be at ease, than He is with many of those who are now in the flames of hell.

It is not because God is unmindful of their wickedness, and does not resent it, that He does not let loose His hand and cut them off. God is not altogether similar to these human beings, although they may imagine Him to be so. The wrath of God burns against them continually; their damnation does not slumber. The pit is prepared; the fire is made ready; the furnace is now hot, ready to receive them; the flames do now rage and glow. The glittering sword is whetted[2] and held over them, and the pit has opened its mouth under them.

The Watchful Serpent

Fifth, the Devil stands ready to fall upon them, and seize them as his own, at whatever moment God will permit him. Sinners belong to him; he has their souls in his possession and under his dominion. The Scripture represents them as his goods. (See Luke 11:21–22.) The devils watch them; they are always at the right hand of these wicked men; they stand waiting for them, like greedy, hungry lions that see their prey and expect to have it, but are for the present kept back.

Now, if God should withdraw His hand, by which the devils are restrained, they would in one moment fly

----

[2] Whetted: sharpened.

upon those poor souls. The old Serpent is gaping for them; hell opens its mouth wide to receive them; and if God should permit it, they would be hastily swallowed up and lost.

The Foundation for Evil

Sixth, consider that, in the souls of wicked men, hellish principles reign, which would immediately kindle and flame out into hellfire, if it were not for God's restraints. There is laid, in the very nature of carnal men, a foundation for the torments of hell. Corrupt principles, reigning in power in them and in full possession of them, are seeds of hellfire.

These principles are active and powerful, and are exceedingly violent in nature. If it were not for the restraining hand of God upon them, they would soon break out; they would flame out in the same manner that the same corruptions, and the same enmity, do in the hearts of damned souls, and they would beget the same torments as they do in those souls.

The souls of the wicked are, in Scripture, compared to the troubled sea: "But the wicked are like the troubled sea, when it cannot rest, whose waters cast up mire and dirt" (Isaiah 57:20). For the present, God restrains their wickedness by His mighty power, as He does the raging waves of the troubled sea, saying, "Hitherto shalt thou come, but no further" (Job 38:11); but if God should withdraw that restraining power, their wickedness would soon overwhelm them.

Sin is the ruin and misery of the soul. It is destructive in its nature; and if God should leave it without restraint, nothing else would be needed to make the soul perfectly miserable. The corruption of the heart of man is immoderate and boundless in its fury; and while wicked men live on this earth, it is like fire pent up by God's restraints. If it were let loose, it would set on fire the whole course of nature.

As the heart is now a cesspool of sin, so if sin were not restrained, it would immediately turn the soul into a fiery oven, or a furnace of fire and brimstone.

The Verge of Eternity

Seventh, it is no security to wicked men—not even for a moment—when they can see no visible means of death at hand. Natural man derives no security from the fact that he is healthy or that he cannot foresee the sudden way in which he will go out of the world. There is no comfort in finding no visible danger in any respect in his circumstances. The manifold and continual experience of the world, in all ages, shows this is no evidence; the world tries to prove that a man is not on the very brink of eternity, and that the next step will not be into another world, but to no avail.

The unseen, unthought-of ways and means by which people suddenly go out of the world are innumerable and inconceivable. Unconverted men walk over the pit of hell on a rotten covering, and there are countless places in this covering that are so weak that the covering will not bear their weight, and these places are not seen. The arrows of death fly unseen at mid-day; the sharpest sight cannot discern them.

God has so many different, un-searchable ways of taking wicked men out of the world and sending them to hell, that there is nothing to indicate that God has to go out of the ordinary course of His providence or perform a miracle, in order to destroy any wicked man, at any moment. All the means by which sinners may go out of the world are so in God's hands, and so univer-sally and absolutely subject to His power and determination, that the fate of sinners would not depend one bit less on the sovereign will of God, if such means were never made use of or never had any bearing on the case.

The Same Natural End for All

Our eighth consideration is that natural man's prudence and care to preserve his own life, or the care of others to preserve him, do not secure him for a moment. Divine providence and universal experience bear testimony to this. Man's own wisdom does not secure him from death; if it were otherwise, we would see some difference between the wise and shrewd men of the world, and others. Perhaps wise men would have less liability to early and unexpected death. But, how is it, in fact? "How dieth the wise man? [Even] as the fool" (Ecclesiastes 2:16).

The Best-Laid Plans

The ninth thing is that all wicked men's pains and contrivances, which they use to escape hell, while they continue to reject Christ and so remain wicked men, do not secure them from hell for even one moment. Almost every natural man who hears of hell flatters himself that he will escape it. He depends on himself for his own security; he flatters himself because of what he has done, what he is now doing, or what he intends to do.

Everyone lays out in his own mind how he will avoid damnation, and flatters himself that he contrives well for himself, and that his schemes will not fail. He may indeed hear that there are few who are saved, and that the greater part of men who have died before him have gone to hell; but each one imagines that he lays out matters for his own escape better than others have done. He does not intend to go to that place of torment; he says within himself that he intends to take effectual care and to order matters for himself so as not to fail.

Even so, the foolish children of men miserably delude themselves in their own schemes, being far too confident in their own strength and wisdom; they trust in nothing but shadows. The greater part of those who, up to the present time, have lived under the same means of grace, and are now dead, have undoubtedly gone to hell. This is not because they were not as wise as those who are now alive; nor was it because they did not lay out matters as well for themselves to secure their own escape.

If we could speak with them and inquire of them, one by one, whether they, when they were alive and when they used to hear about hell, ever expected to be the subjects of misery, we doubtless would hear them reply: "No, I never intended to come here. I had laid out matters otherwise in my mind; I thought I had contrived well for myself; I thought my scheme had been good. I intended to take effectual care, but death came upon me unexpectedly. I did not look for it at that time, or in that manner; it came as a thief. Death outwitted me; God's wrath was too quick for me. Oh, my cursed foolishness! I was flattering myself and pleasing myself with vain dreams of what I would do hereafter; and when I was saying, 'Peace and safety,' then sudden destruction came upon me." (See 1 Thessalonians 5:3.)

The Covenant of Grace

God has placed Himself under no obligation, by any promise, to keep any natural man out of hell. God certainly has made no promises, either of eternal life or of any deliverance or preservation from eternal death, except those that are contained in the covenant of grace, the promises that are given in Christ, in whom all the promises are yea and amen. (See 2 Corinthians 1:20.) But, surely, they who are not the children of the covenant, who do not believe in any of the promises, and who have no interest in the Mediator of the covenant, have no interest in the promises of the covenant of grace.

Consequently, whatever some people have imagined and pretended to understand about the promises made to natural men's earnest seeking and knocking, it is clear and manifest that, whatever pains a natural man takes in religion, whatever prayers he makes, until he believes in Christ, God is under no manner of obligation to keep him from eternal destruction for even a moment.

Thus it is that natural men are held in the hand of God, over the pit of hell; they have deserved the fiery pit, and are already sentenced to it; and God is dreadfully provoked. His anger is as great toward them as it is toward those who are actually suffering the executions and fierceness of His wrath in hell. These natural men have done nothing at all to appease or abate that anger, and God is not in the least bound by any promise to hold them up.

The Devil is waiting for them; hell is gaping for them; the flames gather and flash about them, and would prefer to lay hold of them and swallow them up. The fire pent up in their own hearts is struggling to break out; and they have no interest in any Mediator. There are no means within reach that can be any security to them. In short, they have no refuge, nothing to take hold of. All that preserves them every moment is the sovereign, all-powerful will, the uncovenanted, unobliged forbearance, of an incensed God.

CHAPTER
TWO

Sinner, Beware!

Now, what significance does this have to our daily lives? Perhaps this awful subject may awaken those who remain unconverted in the church, for what you have read is the case of everyone who is out of Christ.

If you are not a child of God, that world of misery, that lake of burning brimstone, is extended abroad under you. Below you is the dreadful pit of the glowing flames of the wrath of God; hell's mouth is gaping wide open; and you have nothing to stand upon, nor anything to take hold of. There is nothing between you and hell except the air; it is only the power and mere pleasure of God that holds you up.

You probably are not aware of this, for although you find you are kept out of hell, you do not see the hand of God in it. Instead, you attribute your current state to other things, such as the health of your body, your care of your own life, and the means you use for your own preservation. But, indeed, these things are nothing; if God should withdraw His hand, they would avail no more to keep you from falling than the thin air can hold up a person who is suspended in it.

Your wickedness makes you as heavy as lead; it drives you down, with great weight and pressure, toward hell. And if God were to let you go, you would immediately sink and swiftly descend and plunge into the bottomless gulf. At that moment, you will see that your health, your own care and prudence, your best contrivance, and all your righteousness, have no more influence to uphold you and keep you out of hell, than a spider's web has to stop a falling rock.

Were it not for the sovereign pleasure of God, the earth would not bear you for one moment, for you are a burden to it. The creation groans with you, "for we know that the whole creation groaneth and travaileth in pain together" (Romans 8:22); creation is unwillingly made subject to the bondage of your corruption.

The sun does not willingly shine upon you to give you light to serve sin and Satan. The earth does not willingly yield her increase to satisfy your lusts, nor is it willingly a stage for your wickedness to be acted upon. The air does not willingly give you breath to maintain the flame of life in your vitals, while you spend your life in the service of God's enemies.

God's creation is good, and was made for men to serve God with, and it does not willingly serve as an instrument to any other purpose. In fact, it groans when it is abused for purposes so directly contrary to its nature and end. The world would spew you out, were it not for the sovereign hand of God.

> *For the creature was made subject to vanity, not willingly, but by reason of him who hath subjected the same in hope, because the creature itself also shall be delivered from the bondage of corruption into the glorious liberty of the children of God.*
> *(Romans 8:20–21)*

The black clouds of God's wrath, full of the dreadful storm and big with thunder, now hang directly over your head; and were it not for the restraining hand of God, His wrath would immediately burst forth upon you. The sovereign pleasure of God, for the present, stays His rough wind; otherwise, it would come with fury, and your destruction would come like a whirlwind, and you would be like the chaff of the summer threshing floor.

The wrath of God is like great waters that are dammed for the present;

they increase more and more, and rise higher and higher, until an outlet is given. The longer the stream is stopped, the more rapid and mighty is its course when at last it is let loose. It is true that judgment against your evil works has not yet been executed; the floods of God's vengeance have been withheld. Nevertheless, your guilt, in the meantime, is constantly increasing, and you are every day storing up more wrath for yourself. (See Romans 2:5.)

The waters are constantly rising and waxing mightier and mightier; and there is nothing but the mere pleasure of God to hold back the waters that press hard to go forward and are unwilling to be stopped. If God were only to withdraw His hand from the floodgate, it would immediately fly open, and the fiery floods of the fierceness and wrath of God would rush forth with inconceivable fury, and would come upon you with omnipotent power. Think of it! If your strength were ten thousand times greater than it is—if it were ten thousand times greater than the strength of the stoutest, sturdiest devil in hell—it would be nothing to withstand or endure the wrath of God.

The bow of God's wrath is bent; the arrow is made ready on the string; and justice bends the arrow at your heart, and strains the bow. It is nothing but the mere pleasure of God, and that of an angry God, without any promise or obligation at all, that keeps the arrow from being made drunk with your blood at every moment.

Therefore, you who have never passed under a great change of heart by the mighty power of the Spirit of God upon your soul; you who never have been born again and been made a new creature (see 2 Corinthians 5:17) and been raised from being dead in sin to a state of newness and previously unexperienced light and life, are in the hands of an angry God.

In whatever way you may have re-formed your life in many respects, and may have had religious inclinations, and may have kept up a form of religion in your family, your prayer closet, and the house of God, it is nothing but God's mere pleasure that keeps you from being this moment swallowed up into everlasting destruction. However unconvinced you may now be of the truth of what you read, perhaps, later on, you will be fully convinced of it.

Note that it was the same for those who have already gone from this world; for destruction came suddenly upon most of them, when they expected nothing of it and while they were saying, "Peace and safety." (See 1 Thessalonians 5:3.) They see now that those things on which they depended for peace and safety were nothing but thin air and empty shadows.

The God who holds you over the pit of hell, as one might hold a spider or some loathsome insect over the fire, abhors you and is dreadfully provoked. His wrath toward you burns like fire; He looks upon you as worthy of nothing else but to be cast into the fire. His eyes are so pure that He cannot bear to have you in His sight; you are ten thousand times more abominable in His eyes than the most hateful, venomous serpent is in ours.

You have offended Him infinitely more than ever a stubborn rebel did his prince; and yet, it is nothing but His hand that holds you from falling into the fire every moment. There is no other reason to be given why you did not go to hell the moment you walked into the house of God on a Sunday morning, provoking His pure eyes by your sinful, wicked manner of attending His solemn worship.

There is no other reason why you did not go to hell last night, or why you were permitted to wake up again in this world, after you had closed your eyes to sleep. And there is no other reason to be given why you have not dropped into hell since you woke up this morning, except that God's hand has held you up. Indeed, there is nothing else that can stand as a reason why you do not this very moment drop down into hell.

O sinner! Consider the fearful danger you are in! It is a great furnace of wrath, a wide and bottomless pit, full of the fire of wrath, over which you are held by the hand of God. And this is the God whose wrath is provoked and incensed as much against you as against many of the damned in hell. You hang by a slender thread, with the flames of divine wrath flashing about it and ready every moment to singe it and burn it asunder; yet you have no interest in any Mediator, and nothing to lay hold of to save yourself, nothing to keep off the flames of wrath, nothing of your own, nothing that you ever have done, nothing that you can do, to induce God to spare you for even a moment.

CHAPTER THREE

A Warning to All

What I have written thus far is not directed only toward those men whom we would look upon and consider as wicked. Rather, my words should serve as a warning to everyone—every man, every woman, and every child. Because all are born into sin, we must take into consideration the following.

Whose Wrath It Is

The wrath of kings is very much dreaded, especially that of absolute monarchs, who have the possessions and lives of their subjects wholly in their power, to be disposed of at their mere will. The Scriptures attest to the terribleness of such wrath:

> *The fear of a king is as the roaring of a lion: whoso provoketh him to anger sinneth against his own soul.* *(Proverbs 20:2)*

However, the wrath that is held against us is the wrath of the infinite God. If it were only the wrath of a man, though he were the most potent ruler of the world, it would be little in comparison.

Anyone who greatly enrages a ruler of this world is liable to undergo the most extreme torments that human cleverness can invent, or that human power can inflict. Even so, the greatest earthly sovereigns, in their greatest majesty and strength, and when clothed in their greatest terrors, are but feeble, despicable worms of the dust, in comparison with the great and almighty Creator and King of heaven and earth.

All the kings of the earth, before God, are as grasshoppers (see Isaiah 40:22): they can do very little, even when they are most enraged and when they have exerted the utmost of their fury. They are nothing, and less than nothing, in comparison with God. Both their love and their hatred are to be despised. The wrath of the great King of Kings is as much more terrible than theirs, as His majesty is greater than theirs.

> *And I say unto you my friends, Be not afraid of them that kill the body, and after that have no more that they can do. But I will forewarn you whom ye shall fear: Fear him, which after he hath killed hath power to cast into hell; yea, I say unto you, Fear him.* (Luke 12:4–5)

The Fierceness of His Wrath

Second, it is the fierceness of His wrath that you are exposed to, as you have sinned against God. We often read of the fury of God, as in Isaiah 59:18: "According to their deeds, accordingly he will repay, fury to his adversaries." The same idea is expressed in Isaiah 66:15:

> *For, behold, the LORD will come with fire, and with his chariots like a whirlwind, to render his anger with fury, and his rebuke with flames of fire.*

We see this in many other places in the Scriptures. In Revelation 19:15, we read of "the winepress of the fierceness and wrath of Almighty God." The words are exceptionally terrible. If only the words "the wrath of God" had been written, it would have implied that which is infinitely dreadful. But it is "the fierceness and wrath of God." The fury of God! The fierceness of Jehovah! Oh, how dreadful that must be! Who can utter or imagine what such expressions carry in them?

Let us examine this verse further. It reads, "the fierceness and wrath of *Almighty* God," as though there would be a very great manifestation of His almighty power in what the fierceness of His wrath would inflict, as though omnipotence would be enraged and exerted, just as men are inclined to exert their strength in the fierceness of their wrath.

Oh, then, what will be the consequence? What will become of the poor worms that will suffer under it? Whose hands can be strong? And whose heart can endure? (See Ezekiel 22:14.) To what a dreadful, inexpressible, inconceivable depth of misery must the poor creature be sunk who becomes the victim of this wrath!

You who remain in an unregenerate state, consider this: the fact that God will execute the fierceness of His anger, implies that He will inflict wrath without any pity. When God beholds the unspeakable extremity of your condition, and sees your torment to be so vastly disproportional to your strength, and how your poor soul is crushed and sinks down, as it were, into an infinite gloom, He will have no compassion upon you; He will not hold back the executions of His wrath, or in the least lighten His hand.

There will be no moderation or mercy, nor will God then at all stay His rough wind. (See Isaiah 27:8.) He will have no regard for your welfare, nor will He be at all concerned about your increasing suffering, except that you will not suffer beyond what strict justice requires. Nothing will be withheld with the reason that it is too hard for you to bear.

> *Therefore will I also deal in fury:*
> *mine eye shall not spare, neither*
> *will I have pity: and though they*
> *cry in mine ears with a loud*
> *voice, yet will I not hear them.*
> *(Ezekiel 8:18)*

Now God stands ready to pity you; this is a day of mercy; you may cry now with some encouragement of obtaining mercy. But, once the day of mercy is past, your most lamentable and miserable cries and shrieks will be in vain; you will be wholly lost and thrown away, and there will be no regard for your welfare.

God will have no other use to put you to, except to suffer misery; you will be allowed to exist for no other end. You will be a vessel of wrath, "fitted to destruction" (Romans 9:22); and there will be no other use for this vessel, except to be filled full of wrath. God will be so far from pitying you when you cry to Him, that He will only laugh at you.

Note what He says in the following passage:

> *Because I have called, and ye refused; I have stretched out my hand, and no man regarded; but ye have set at nought all my counsel, and would none of my reproof: I also will laugh at your*

*calamity; I will mock when your
fear cometh; when your fear
cometh as desolation, and your
destruction cometh as a whirlwind; when distress and an-
guish cometh upon you. Then
shall they call upon me, but I
will not answer; they shall seek
me early, but they shall not find
me: for that they hated knowledge, and did not choose the fear
of the LORD: they would none of
my counsel: they despised all my
reproof. Therefore shall they eat
of the fruit of their own way, and
be filled with their own devices.
For the turning away of the sim-
ple shall slay them, and the
prosperity of fools shall destroy
them. But whoso hearkeneth
unto me shall dwell safely, and
shall be quiet from fear of evil.*
(Proverbs 1:24–33)

How awful are those words, also,
from Isaiah 63:3, which are the words
of the great God:

I will tread them in mine anger, and trample them in my fury; and their blood shall be sprinkled upon my garments, and I will stain all my raiment.

It is, perhaps, impossible to imagine words that carry in them greater manifestations of these three things: contempt, hatred, and fierceness of indignation. If you cry to God to pity you, He will be so far from pitying you in your downcast state or from showing you the least regard or favor, that, instead of that, He will only tread you underfoot. And, although He will know that you cannot bear the weight of omnipotence treading upon you, He will not regard that, but He will crush you under His feet without mercy.

Indeed, He will crush out your blood and make it fly, and it will be sprinkled on His garments, so as to stain all His clothing. He will not only hate you, but He will hold you in the utmost contempt: no place will be thought fit for you, except under His feet, to be trodden down as the mire of the streets.

The Resulting Misery

Third, the misery to which you are exposed is that which God will inflict for the very purpose of showing what that wrath of Jehovah is. God has had it on His heart to show to angels and men not only how excellent His love is, but also how terrible His wrath is.

Sometimes earthly kings have a mind to show how terrible their wrath is, by the extreme punishments they execute on those who provoke them. Nebuchadnezzar, that mighty and haughty monarch of the Chaldean empire, was willing to show his wrath when he was enraged with Shadrach, Meshach, and Abednego. (See Daniel 3.) Accordingly, he gave orders that the burning fiery furnace should be heated seven times hotter than it ever was before (see verse 19); doubtless, it was raised to the utmost degree of fierceness that human ingenuity could raise it.

Like Nebuchadnezzar, the great God is also willing to show His wrath, and to magnify His awful majesty and mighty power in the extreme sufferings of His enemies. Notice what is written in Romans 9:22:

> *What if God, willing to show his wrath, and to make his power known, endured with much longsuffering the vessels of wrath fitted to destruction?*

And, seeing that this is what He has determined—even to show how terrible the unrestrained wrath, the fury, and the fierceness of Jehovah is—He will carry it out to its fulfillment.

This will be something accomplished and brought to pass that will be dreadful to any witness of it. When the great and angry God has risen up and executed His awful vengeance on a poor sinner, and the wretch is actually suffering the infinite weight and power of His indignation, then God will call upon the whole universe to behold the awful majesty and mighty power that is to be seen in it.

> *And the people shall be as the burnings of lime: as thorns cut up shall they be burned in the fire. Hear, ye that are far off, what I have done; and, ye that are near, acknowledge my might. The sinners in Zion are afraid; fearfulness hath surprised the hypocrites. (Isaiah 33:12–14)*

It will be the same with you who are in an unconverted state, if you continue in it. The infinite might and majesty and terribleness of the omnipotent God will be magnified upon you, in the unspeakable intensity of your torments. You will be tormented in the presence of the holy angels, and in the presence of the Lamb; and when you are in this state of suffering, the glorious inhabitants of heaven will go forth and look on the awful spectacle, that they may see what the wrath and fierceness of the Almighty is. Then, when they have seen it, they will fall down and adore that great power and majesty.

Read from the Scriptures in Isaiah 66:23–24:

And it shall come to pass, that from one new moon to another, and from one sabbath to another, shall all flesh come to worship before me, saith the LORD. And they shall go forth, and look upon the carcases of the men that have transgressed against me: for their worm shall not die, neither shall their fire be quenched; and they shall be an abhorring unto all flesh.

Certainly, this is worth your consideration even now, for "all have sinned, and come short of the glory of God" (Romans 3:23).

An Everlasting Torment

The fourth thing you must consider is that the wrath of God is an everlasting wrath. It would be dreadful to suffer this "fierceness and wrath of Almighty God" (Revelation 19:15) for just one moment; but you must suffer it for all eternity. There will be no end to this exquisitely horrible misery. When you look forward, you will see a long forever, a boundless duration before you, which will swallow up your thoughts and amaze your soul; and you will absolutely lose all hope or confidence of ever having any deliverance, any end, any mitigation, any rest at all.

You will know without question that you must wear out long ages, millions and millions of ages, in wrestling and conflicting with this almighty, merciless vengeance. And then, when you have done so, when so many ages have actually been spent by you in this manner, you will know that everything you have suffered is but a pinpoint compared with what remains. Your punishment will indeed be infinite.

Oh, who can express what the state of a soul in such circumstances is! All that we can possibly say about it, gives but a very feeble, faint representation of it; it is inexpressible and inconceivable, for "who knoweth the power of [God's] anger" (Psalm 90:11)?

How dreadful is the state of those who are daily and hourly in danger of this great wrath and infinite misery! Nevertheless, this is the dismal case of all souls reading this who have not been born again, however moral and strict, sober and religious, they may otherwise be. Oh, that you would consider it, whether you are young or old!

There is reason to think that there are many now reading this book, who will actually be the subjects of this very misery for all eternity. I do not know who they are, or in what places they now sit, or what thoughts they now have. It may be that they are now at ease, and read all these things without much disturbance, and are now flattering themselves that they are not the people in great jeopardy, promising themselves that they will escape.

If we knew that there was one person, and only one, among all our friends and neighbors, who was to be the subject of this misery, what an awful thing it would be to think of! If we knew who it was, what an awful sight it would be to see such a person! How all the rest of our friends and neighbors would lift up a lamentable and bitter cry over him!

But, alas! instead of one, how many are likely to remember reading this book once they are in hell? It would be no great wonder to me if some who read this should be in hell in a very short time, even before this year is out. And it would be no wonder if some people, who now sit in health, quiet and secure, should be there before tomorrow morning. And, finally, those of you who continue in a natural condition, who will keep out of hell longest, will be there in just a little time! Your damnation does not slumber; it will come swiftly and, in all probability, very suddenly upon many of you. You have reason to marvel that you are not already in hell.

This, doubtless, has been the case of some people whom you have seen and known, who never deserved hell more than you, and who had every reason to believe they would be alive today, just as you are. Their case is past all hope; they are crying in extreme misery and perfect despair; but you are in the land of the living, and you have an opportunity to obtain salvation. What would those poor, damned, hopeless souls not give for one day's opportunity such as you now enjoy?

A Final Call to Salvation

And now, you have an extraordinary opportunity, a day wherein Christ has thrown the door of mercy wide open, and stands calling and crying with a loud voice to poor sinners; a day wherein many are flocking to Him, and pressing into the kingdom of God. Many are daily coming from the east, west, north, and south. Many who were very recently in the same miserable condition that you are in, are now in a happy state, with their hearts filled with love for Him who has loved them and washed them from their sins in His own blood; they are rejoicing "in [the] hope of the glory of God" (Romans 5:2).

How awful it is to be left behind on such a day! How horrible to see so many others feasting, while you are pining and perishing! How dreadful to see so many rejoicing and singing for joy of heart, while you have cause to mourn for sorrow of heart, and to howl for vexation of spirit! How can you rest one moment in such a condition? Are your souls not as precious as the souls of the people who are flocking to Christ every day?

Do you not know many people who have lived long in the world, and are not, even to this day, born again? They are aliens from the commonwealth of Israel, and have done nothing, ever since they were born, except treasure up wrath against the day of wrath, just as the apostle wrote in Romans 2:5:

But after thy hardness and impenitent heart treasurest up unto thyself wrath against the day of wrath and revelation of the righteous judgment of God.

Oh, dear reader, if you have not yet turned to Christ, even in your later years, then your case, especially, is extremely dangerous. Your guilt and hardness of heart are extremely great. Do you not see how people of your years are generally passed over and left, in the remarkable and wonderful dispensation of God's mercy? You must carefully consider your condition, and awaken thoroughly out of sleep. You cannot bear the fierceness and wrath of the infinite God.

And you, young men and young women, will you neglect this precious season that you now enjoy, when so many others of your age are renouncing all youthful vanities and flocking to Christ? You, especially now, have an extraordinary opportunity; but if you neglect it, it will soon be with you as it was with those who spent all the precious days of youth in sin, and are now in such a dreadful state of blindness and hardness.

And you, children, who are unconverted, do you not know that you are going down to hell, to bear the dreadful wrath of that God who is now angry with you every day and every night? Will you be content to be the children of the Devil, when so many other children in the world have been converted, and are the holy and happy children of the King of Kings?

Let all who are yet out of Christ, and hanging over the pit of hell, whether they be old men and women, or middle-aged, or young people, or little children, now hearken to the loud calls of God's Word and His providence. This acceptable year of the Lord, a day of such great favor to some, will doubtless be a day of as remarkable vengeance to others.

Men's hearts harden, and their guilt increases rapidly, in times such as these, if they neglect their souls; and never has there been so great a danger of such people being given up to hardness of heart and blindness of mind. God seems now to be hastily gathering in His elect in all parts of the world.

Most likely, the greater part of adults who will ever be saved, will be brought in now in a short period of time, and it will be as it was during the great outpouring of the Spirit upon the Jews in the apostles' days. The elect will obtain His Spirit, and the rest will be blinded. If this should be the case with you, you will eternally curse this day, and will curse the day that ever you were born, to see such a season of the pouring out of God's Spirit. You will wish that you had died and gone to hell before you had seen it.

Now, undoubtedly, it is as it was in the days of John the Baptist:

> *The ax is laid unto the root of the trees: therefore every tree which bringeth not forth good fruit is hewn down, and cast into the fire.* (Matthew 3:10)

Therefore, let everyone who is out of Christ, now awaken and fly from the wrath to come. The wrath of Almighty God is now undoubtedly hanging over a great number of you. Let everyone fly out of Sodom:

> *Escape for thy life; look not behind thee, neither stay thou in all the plain; escape to the mountain, lest thou be consumed.* (Genesis 19:17)